Scholastic Phonics

Helpful Plants

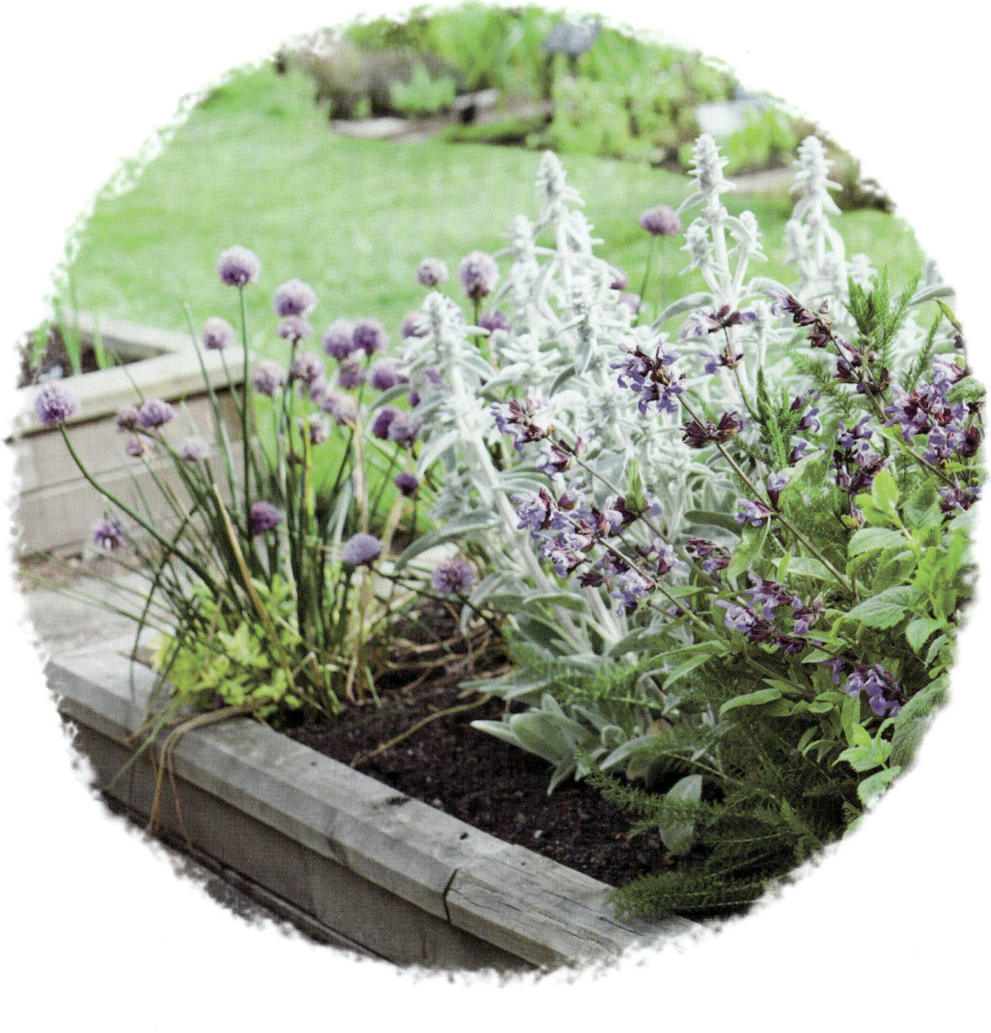

Published in the UK by Scholastic Education, 2023
Scholastic Distribution Centre, Bosworth Avenue, Tournament Fields, Warwick, CV34 6UQ
Scholastic Ireland, 89E Lagan Road, Dublin Industrial Estate, Glasnevin, Dublin, D11 HP5F

SCHOLASTIC and associated logos are trademarks and/or registered trademarks of Scholastic Inc.
www.scholastic.co.uk
© 2023 Scholastic
1 2 3 4 5 6 7 8 9   3 4 5 6 7 8 9 0 1 2

Printed by Ashford Colour Press
The book is made of materials from well-managed, FSC®-certified forests and other controlled sources.

A CIP catalogue record for this book is available from the British Library.
ISBN 978-0702-32114-6

All rights reserved. This book is sold subject to the condition that it shall not, by way of trade or otherwise, be lent, hired out or otherwise circulated in any form of binding or cover other than that in which it is published. No part of this publication may be reproduced, stored in a retrieval system, or transmitted in any form or by any other means (electronic, mechanical, photocopying, recording or otherwise) without prior written permission of Scholastic.

Every effort has been made to trace copyright holders for the works reproduced in this publication, and the publishers apologise for any inadvertent omissions.

Author
Alice Hemming
Editorial team
Rachel Morgan, Vicki Yates, Fiona Undrill, Jennie Clifford
Design team
Dipa Mistry, Andrea Lewis, We Are Grace
Photographs
Cover georgeclerk/iStock
p4 Pressmaster/Shutterstock
p5 (cotton plant) Jerry Horbert/Shutterstock
p5 (boy) len4foto/iStock
p6 Hakase_420/Shutterstock
p7, 24 New Africa/Shutterstock
p7 (lightbulb) VectorCookies/iStock
p8 PattPaulStudio/Shutterstock
p9 Orawan Pattarawimonchai/Shutterstock
p9, 21 (warning triangle) Fourleaflover/iStock
p10–11 schankz/Shutterstock
p12 Olya Humeniuk/Shutterstock
p1, 13, 24 (outside planter) JoannaTkaczuk/Shutterstock
p13 (inside pots) Carlos Amarillo/Shutterstock
p3, 14 Yala/Shutterstock
p15 (ice cube) Khomulo Anna/Shutterstock
p15 (girl) Lyubov Kobyakova/Shutterstock
p16 owngarden/iStock
p17 mahey/Shutterstock
p18–19 payamona/iStock
p20, 24 Olga_Ionina/Shutterstock
p21 Georgy Dzyura/Shutterstock
p22 NDAB Creativity/Shutterstock
p23 baona/iStock

Help your child to read!

This book practises these letters and letter sounds.
Point and say the sounds with your child:

- u (as in 'helpful')
- oul (as in 'could')
- oor (as in 'indoors')
- al (as in 'stalks')
- tch (as in 'itch')
- a (as in 'plant')
- sc (as in 'scent')

Your child may need help to read these common tricky words:

- are
- people
- of
- your
- to
- their
- the
- our
- many
- anything
- eyes
- they

Before reading
- Look at the cover picture and read the title together.
  Read the back cover blurb to your child.
- Ask your child: *What do you think it means by 'helpful' plants?
  Can you think of any ways a plant could be helpful?*
- Talk about the image in the magnifying glass.

During reading
- If your child gets stuck on a word, remind them to sound
  it out and then blend the sounds to read the word: p-l-a-n-t, plant.
- If they are still stuck, show them how to read the word.
- Enjoy looking at the pictures together. Pause to talk about the information.

After reading
- Talk about the images on page 24. What can your child tell you about them?
- Ask your child: *Which ways were plants helpful in the book?*
- Talk to your child about whether they've tried gardening or
  keeping houseplants.

Plants are helpful! No creature could survive without plants. People use plants for food, fuel, clothes and houses.

This plant is cotton.

Some of your clothes could be made of cotton.

Plants help animals to live. Their leaves help make the air we need to live.

In our homes, the air may carry chemicals from cleaning products we use. Some indoor plants can help clean the air.

💡 Bamboo cleans the air.

Scientists make many modern medicines from plants.

We can use some plants at home. Gel from aloe stalks soothes minor burns.

⚠ Never put anything on your skin without checking with an adult.

Bees collect nectar from flowers to make honey.

The scent and appearance of flowers attracts bees. Bees spread pollen from plant to plant.

Bugs can be helpful, but some can give us itchy bites.

The strong scent of lavender, basil or mint can keep bugs away.

Herb planters make nice features outdoors or indoors.

You could eat the herbs you grow, or put them in drinks.

Cut the stalks off mint and freeze the leaves for a tasty way to cool a glass of water.

In the kitchen, we cook with all sorts of plants, like fruit and vegetables, as well as herbs.

Without plants, there would be no food. Even meat comes from animals which eat plants.

Plants are not always helpful.

Hayfever is a pollen allergy, which makes people sneeze and their eyes itch.

Some plants can be harmful to eat or walk past.

Nettles sting and itch.

Hogweed could give you burns and blisters. Hogweed can grow to the size of an elephant!

⚠ Stay away from plants you don't recognise.

Scientists say walking outdoors and enjoying nature is good for lowering stress levels.